Crafted by

**Brilliant
Planners**

This Anxiety Workbook Belongs to:

_____

How Will This Planner Help You

Brilliant Planners' Anxiety Workbook is the perfect way to fight anxiety and manage your worries before they take control over you. This journal is designed to guide you through and towards developing a mentality and practice of saving a few minutes each week to re-frame your thoughts, indentifying the sources of your anxiety, get in the habit of positive thinking, and prioritizing your mental health. It's devided into 3 months and in each month, there are monthly and weekly activities.

Features:

Self Care Calendar
Thought tracker
Affirmations
My Resources
My Quotes
My Happy Place
Weekly Check In
Stress Reduction
Positive Thinking
Balance Wheel
Self Care Goals
My Action Plan
My Triggers
Notes

Month

_____

Self Care Calendar

Month: _____

◯ Do a 5 min breathing exercice	◯ Make a feel good playlist	◯ Brainstorm new activities to try	◯ Watch your favourite movie	◯ Listen to a podcast
◯ Go for a walk	◯ Declutter your space	◯ Read an inspiring book	◯ Write down 5 things to be happy about right now	◯ Stretch out your body
◯ Cook your favorite meal	◯ Dance it out	◯ Take a long shower or bubble bath	◯ Enjoy your favorite beverage	◯ Ask someone about their day
◯ Have a pamper session	◯ Call a friend	◯ Have a digital detox day	◯ Make time for creativity	◯ Write down your thoughts & feelings
◯ Say affirmations out loud	◯ Indulge in your favorite food	◯ Compliment someone	◯ Write down 3 things you love about yourself	◯ Enjoy a meal distraction free
◯ Drink more water today	◯ Try a new workout	◯ Clean out a junk drawer	◯ Sleep in or go to bed early	◯ Celebrate a small win

Thought Tracker

Month: _____

Worrying about the Future

In this exercice, be mindful of every time you find your mind dwelling in the future, worrying about an event or situation that may or may not happen. If this is a legitimate problem that needs addressing, devote time to it to find a solution, but if this is a thought that is a result of fear or worry, fill out an entry in this journal table.

Thought/Worry	Is this something that is for sure going to happen?	What, if anything, can be done about it?
	○ Yes ○ No ○ Maybe	
	○ Yes ○ No ○ Maybe	
	○ Yes ○ No ○ Maybe	
	○ Yes ○ No ○ Maybe	
	○ Yes ○ No ○ Maybe	
	○ Yes ○ No ○ Maybe	
	○ Yes ○ No ○ Maybe	
	○ Yes ○ No ○ Maybe	
	○ Yes ○ No ○ Maybe	
	○ Yes ○ No ○ Maybe	
	○ Yes ○ No ○ Maybe	
	○ Yes ○ No ○ Maybe	
	○ Yes ○ No ○ Maybe	
	○ Yes ○ No ○ Maybe	
	○ Yes ○ No ○ Maybe	
	○ Yes ○ No ○ Maybe	
	○ Yes ○ No ○ Maybe	
	○ Yes ○ No ○ Maybe	
	○ Yes ○ No ○ Maybe	
	○ Yes ○ No ○ Maybe	
	○ Yes ○ No ○ Maybe	
	○ Yes ○ No ○ Maybe	
	○ Yes ○ No ○ Maybe	
	○ Yes ○ No ○ Maybe	

Affirmations

Month: _____

1. _____
2. _____
3. _____
4. _____
5. _____
6. _____
7. _____
8. _____
9. _____
10. _____
11. _____
12. _____
13. _____
14. _____
15. _____
16. _____
17. _____
18. _____
19. _____
20. _____
21. _____
22. _____
23. _____
24. _____
25. _____
26. _____
27. _____
28. _____

My Resources

Month: _____

Books

_____

_____

_____

_____

Movies

_____

_____

_____

_____

Video Games

_____

_____

_____

_____

Music

_____

_____

_____

_____

TV Shows

_____

_____

_____

_____

My Resources

Month: _____

Books

Movies

Video Games

Music

TV Shows

My Quotes

○ _____
○ _____
○ _____
○ _____
○ _____
○ _____
○ _____
○ _____
○ _____
○ _____
○ _____

My Quotes

Month: _____

○ ....
○ ....
○ ....
○ ....
○ ....
○ ....
○ ....
○ ....
○ ....
○ ....
○ ....

My Happy Place

Bad days are horrible. Why? Because somehow, it puts into focus all of the wrong things that are suddenly happening in your life.

But here's an important reminder:
It's only temporary.

You won't be feeling like this forever. So let's take a minute to do a grounding exercice. Let's go to your happy place and remind yourself of the things you can control.

On the next page, list down all of the things that give you the most comfort and joy.

Write down your guilty pleasures, favorite songs, pictures, and quotes that make you smile, recipes for your favorite go-to meal, or anything that will help lift you up when a bad day comes.

The next time you're having a bad day, you have a list in hand that will help you feel better immediately.

My Happy Place

Month: _____

My Favorite Hobbies

- ○ _____
- ○ _____
- ○ _____
- ○ _____
- ○ _____

My Favorite Songs

- ○ _____
- ○ _____
- ○ _____
- ○ _____
- ○ _____

My Favorite Movies/TV Shows

- ○ _____
- ○ _____
- ○ _____
- ○ _____
- ○ _____

My Favorite Foods

- ○ _____
- ○ _____
- ○ _____
- ○ _____
- ○ _____

My Favorite Books

- ○ _____
- ○ _____
- ○ _____
- ○ _____
- ○ _____

My Favorite Routine

_____
_____
_____
_____
_____

Things that cheer me up

- ○ _____
- ○ _____
- ○ _____
- ○ _____
- ○ _____

Weekly Check In

Often, our biggest problems come from a lack of self-awareness.

Burn-out, panic, and anxiety attacks — even depression is caused by a profound disconnect with our authentic selves.

But when we know who we are — our needs, desires, and how we truly feel — we make better decisions and manifest positive changes in our life.

A mood tracker is a powerful tool for self-awareness. It emphasizes what activities work for you and what doesn't.

Still, it also helps you define any negative stressors you didn't know you have.

This worksheet will help you track your mood on bad days to be more in tune with your self-care needs.

Weekly Check In

Week: _____

Health: ♡ ♡ ♡ ♡ ♡   Love: ♡ ♡ ♡ ♡ ♡

Emotions: ♡ ♡ ♡ ♡ ♡   Energy: ♡ ♡ ♡ ♡ ♡

Career: ♡ ♡ ♡ ♡ ♡   Fun: ♡ ♡ ♡ ♡ ♡

Passion: ♡ ♡ ♡ ♡ ♡   Social: ♡ ♡ ♡ ♡ ♡

How am I feeling and why?

_____

_____

_____

_____

_____

_____

_____

_____

Something good about this week

_____

_____

_____

_____

_____

_____

_____

_____

_____

_____

_____

_____

Something that was on my mind?

_____

_____

_____

_____

_____

Stress Reduction

Week: _____

Goal #1: _____

Action Steps

○ _____   ○ _____
○ _____   ○ _____
○ _____   ○ _____
○ _____   ○ _____

Check-In / Results

Dates	Notes

Goal #2: _____

Action Steps

○ _____   ○ _____
○ _____   ○ _____
○ _____   ○ _____
○ _____   ○ _____

Check-In / Results

Dates	Notes

Positive Thinking

Having negative thoughts is entirely reasonable. It's a natural human instinct, linked to our fight -or- flight response.

In fact, negative thoughts are beneficial in our decision-making process and can help us establish healthy boundaries.

However, too much of it can lead to unnecessary stress. While it's essential to acknowledge your negative thoughts, it's also crucial to challenge them when they impair your judgement.

If you allow negative thoughts to take up permanent space, you'll end up living a toxic and unhealthy life.

The next Positive Thinking page is designed to help you navigate your thoughts and feelings.

Positive Thinking

Week: _____

Negative Thoughts

_____

_____

_____

Is this thought true and do I have evidence that this is true

_____

_____

_____

Am I blaming someone else without taking accountability

_____

_____

_____

Am I having this thought because I'm unhappy about something else

_____

_____

_____

Positive Thoughts

_____

_____

_____

Balance Wheel

It's time to create a plan to help you achieve your goals, manage your expectations, and know what to prioritize.

A balance wheel is an excellent way to do just that.

It's a simple but potent self-assessment tool that will give you a clear visual presentationof how balanced your life is now.

At the same time, it shows you how to improve for the future.

Balance Wheel

Week: _____

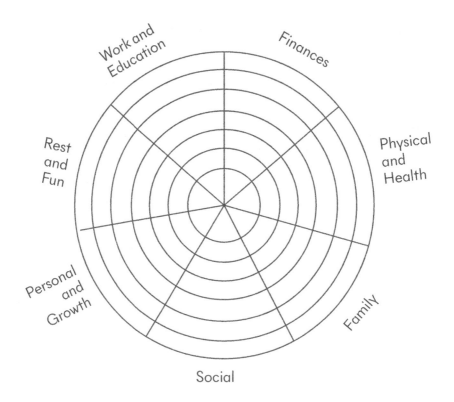

Positive Thoughts

Work and Education: _____

Finances: _____

Physical and Health: _____

Family: _____

Social: _____

Personal Growth: _____

Rest and Fun: _____

My Action Plan

First Things First

When it comes to establishing a routine that works, the most critical step is to develop clear goals.

How many times have you forgotten to do something for yourself? Self-care is particularly challenging because we don't inherently have the habit of choosing ourselves first.

Many of us struggle because we get so caught up with different priorities — our careers, family, social lives — that we subconsciously put ourselves in the backburner.

To start creating new healthy ones that would allow you to take better care of yourself, you first need to establish clear self-care goals.

My Action Plan

Week: _____

What is your worry?

_____
_____
_____
_____
_____
_____

What are some ways you can calm yourself with?

_____
_____
_____
_____

What positive result will you have from taking action?

_____
_____
_____
_____
_____

What is your worry trying to protect you from?

_____
_____
_____
_____
_____
_____
_____
_____
_____

What action will you take to manage this worry?

_____
_____
_____
_____
_____
_____
_____

My Triggers

Week: _____

Why do these triggers make you feel anxious?

_____
_____
_____
_____
_____
_____

What are current strategies to manage these triggers?

_____
_____
_____
_____
_____
_____

How will you feel when you overcome these triggers?

_____
_____
_____
_____

My Happy Place

Month: _____

My Favorite Hobbies

○ _____
○ _____
○ _____
○ _____
○ _____

My Favorite Songs

○ _____
○ _____
○ _____
○ _____
○ _____

My Favorite Movies/TV Shows

○ _____
○ _____
○ _____
○ _____
○ _____

My Favorite Foods

○ _____
○ _____
○ _____
○ _____
○ _____

My Favorite Books

○ _____
○ _____
○ _____
○ _____
○ _____

My Favorite Routine

_____
_____
_____
_____
_____
_____
_____
_____

Things that cheer me up

○ _____
○ _____
○ _____
○ _____
○ _____

Weekly Check In

Week: _____

Health: ♡ ♡ ♡ ♡ ♡	Love: ♡ ♡ ♡ ♡ ♡	
Emotions: ♡ ♡ ♡ ♡ ♡	Energy: ♡ ♡ ♡ ♡ ♡	
Career: ♡ ♡ ♡ ♡ ♡	Fun: ♡ ♡ ♡ ♡ ♡	
Passion: ♡ ♡ ♡ ♡ ♡	Social: ♡ ♡ ♡ ♡ ♡	

How am I feeling and why?

_____
_____
_____
_____
_____
_____
_____
_____
_____

Something good about this week

_____
_____
_____
_____
_____
_____
_____
_____
_____
_____
_____
_____

Something that was on my mind?

_____
_____
_____
_____

Stress Reduction

Week: _____

Goal #1: _____

Action Steps

○ _____   ○ _____
○ _____   ○ _____
○ _____   ○ _____
○ _____   ○ _____

Check-In / Results

Dates	Notes

Goal #2: _____

Action Steps

○ _____   ○ _____
○ _____   ○ _____
○ _____   ○ _____
○ _____   ○ _____

Check-In / Results

Dates	Notes

Positive Thinking

Week: _____

Negative Thoughts

_____

_____

_____

Is this thought true and do I have evidence that this is true

_____

_____

_____

Am I blaming someone else without taking accountability

_____

_____

_____

Am I having this thought because I'm unhappy about something else

_____

_____

_____

Positive Thoughts

_____

_____

_____

Balance Wheel

Week: _____

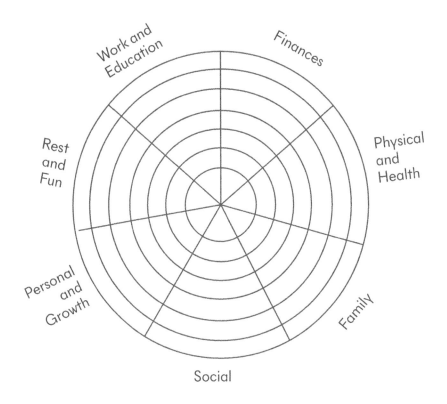

Positive Thoughts

Work and Education: _____

Finances: _____

Physical and Health: _____

Family: _____

Social: _____

Personal Growth: _____

Rest and Fun: _____

My Action Plan

Week: _____

What is your worry?

_____
_____
_____
_____
_____
_____
_____

What is your worry trying to protect you from?

_____
_____
_____
_____
_____
_____
_____
_____
_____

What are some ways you can calm yourself with?

_____
_____
_____
_____

What action will you take to manage this worry?

_____
_____
_____

What positive result will you have from taking action?

_____
_____
_____
_____
_____
_____

My Triggers

Why do these triggers make you feel anxious?

_____

_____

_____

_____

_____

_____

_____

_____

What are current strategies to manage these triggers?

_____

_____

_____

_____

_____

_____

_____

_____

How will you feel when you overcome these triggers?

_____

_____

_____

_____

_____

_____

_____

My Happy Place

Month: _____

My Favorite Hobbies

○ _____
○ _____
○ _____
○ _____
○ _____

My Favorite Songs

○ _____
○ _____
○ _____
○ _____
○ _____

My Favorite Movies/TV Shows

○ _____
○ _____
○ _____
○ _____
○ _____

My Favorite Foods

○ _____
○ _____
○ _____
○ _____
○ _____

My Favorite Books

○ _____
○ _____
○ _____
○ _____
○ _____

My Favorite Routine

_____
_____
_____
_____
_____
_____

Things that cheer me up

○ _____
○ _____
○ _____
○ _____
○ _____

Weekly Check In

Week: _____

Health: ♡ ♡ ♡ ♡ ♡ Love: ♡ ♡ ♡ ♡ ♡

Emotions: ♡ ♡ ♡ ♡ ♡ Energy: ♡ ♡ ♡ ♡ ♡

Career: ♡ ♡ ♡ ♡ ♡ Fun: ♡ ♡ ♡ ♡ ♡

Passion: ♡ ♡ ♡ ♡ ♡ Social: ♡ ♡ ♡ ♡ ♡

How am I feeling and why?

Something good about this week

_____
_____
_____
_____
_____
_____
_____
_____
_____
_____
_____

Something that was on my mind?

_____
_____
_____
_____

Stress Reduction

Week: _____

Goal #1: _____

Action Steps

○ _____   ○ _____
○ _____   ○ _____
○ _____   ○ _____
○ _____   ○ _____

Check-In / Results

Dates	Notes

Goal #2: _____

Action Steps

○ _____   ○ _____
○ _____   ○ _____
○ _____   ○ _____
○ _____   ○ _____

Check-In / Results

Dates	Notes

Positive Thinking

Week: _____

Negative Thoughts

_____

_____

_____

Is this thought true and do I have evidence that this is true

_____

_____

_____

Am I blaming someone else without taking accountability

_____

_____

_____

Am I having this thought because I'm unhappy about something else

_____

_____

_____

Positive Thoughts

_____

_____

_____

Balance Wheel

Week: _____

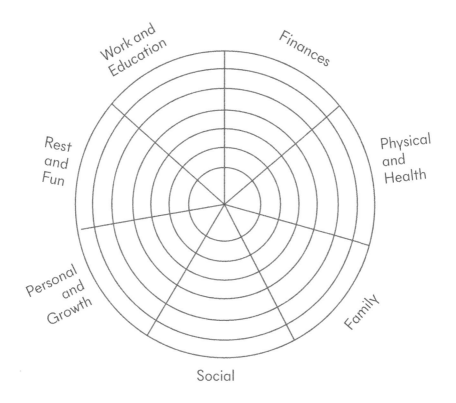

Positive Thoughts

Work and Education: _____

Finances: _____

Physical and Health: _____

Family: _____

Social: _____

Personal Growth: _____

Rest and Fun: _____

My Action Plan

Week: _____

What is your worry?

_____
_____
_____
_____
_____
_____
_____

What is your worry trying to protect you from?

_____
_____
_____
_____
_____
_____
_____
_____
_____

What are some ways you can calm yourself with?

_____
_____
_____
_____
_____

What action will you take to manage this worry?

_____
_____

What positive result will you have from taking action?

_____
_____
_____
_____
_____
_____

_____
_____
_____
_____
_____
_____

My Triggers

Week: _____

Why do these triggers make you feel anxious?

_____

_____

_____

_____

_____

_____

_____

What are current strategies to manage these triggers?

_____

_____

_____

_____

_____

_____

How will you feel when you overcome these triggers?

_____

_____

_____

_____

_____

_____

My Happy Place

Month: _____

My Favorite Hobbies

○ _____
○ _____
○ _____
○ _____
○ _____

My Favorite Songs

○ _____
○ _____
○ _____
○ _____
○ _____

My Favorite Movies/TV Shows

○ _____
○ _____
○ _____
○ _____
○ _____

My Favorite Foods

○ _____
○ _____
○ _____
○ _____
○ _____

My Favorite Books

○ _____
○ _____
○ _____
○ _____
○ _____

My Favorite Routine

_____
_____
_____
_____
_____
_____
_____
_____

Things that cheer me up

○ _____
○ _____
○ _____
○ _____
○ _____

Weekly Check In

Week: _____

Health: ♡ ♡ ♡ ♡ ♡   Love: ♡ ♡ ♡ ♡ ♡

Emotions: ♡ ♡ ♡ ♡ ♡   Energy: ♡ ♡ ♡ ♡ ♡

Career: ♡ ♡ ♡ ♡ ♡   Fun: ♡ ♡ ♡ ♡ ♡

Passion: ♡ ♡ ♡ ♡ ♡   Social: ♡ ♡ ♡ ♡ ♡

How am I feeling and why?

_____
_____
_____
_____
_____
_____
_____
_____
_____
_____

Something good about this week

_____
_____
_____
_____
_____
_____
_____
_____
_____
_____
_____
_____
_____
_____

Something that was on my mind?

_____
_____
_____
_____

Stress Reduction

Week: _____

Goal #1: _____

Action Steps

○ _____   ○ _____
○ _____   ○ _____
○ _____   ○ _____
○ _____   ○ _____

Check-In / Results

Dates	Notes

Goal #2: _____

Action Steps

○ _____   ○ _____
○ _____   ○ _____
○ _____   ○ _____
○ _____   ○ _____

Check-In / Results

Dates	Notes

Positive Thinking

Week: _____

Negative Thoughts

_____
_____
_____

Is this thought true and do I have evidence that this is true

_____
_____
_____

Am I blaming someone else without taking accountability

_____
_____
_____

Am I having this thought because I'm unhappy about something else

_____
_____
_____

Positive Thoughts

_____
_____
_____

Balance Wheel

Week: _____

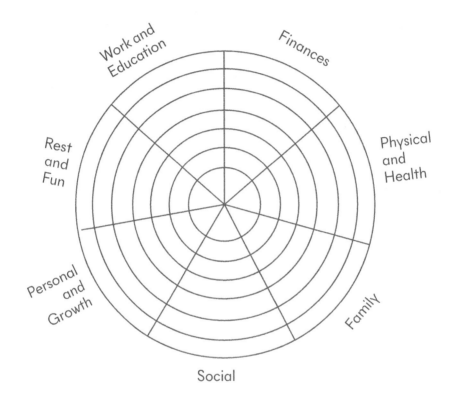

Positive Thoughts

Work and Education: _____

Finances: _____

Physical and Health: _____

Family: _____

Social: _____

Personal Growth: _____

Rest and Fun: _____

My Action Plan

Week: _____

What is your worry?

_____
_____
_____
_____
_____
_____
_____

What is your worry trying to protect you from?

_____
_____
_____
_____
_____
_____
_____
_____

What are some ways you can calm yourself with?

_____
_____
_____
_____

What action will you take to manage this worry?

_____
_____
_____

What positive result will you have from taking action?

_____
_____
_____
_____
_____

_____
_____
_____
_____
_____

My Triggers

Why do these triggers make you feel anxious?

_____

_____

_____

_____

_____

_____

_____

What are current strategies to manage these triggers?

_____

_____

_____

_____

_____

_____

_____

How will you feel when you overcome these triggers?

_____

_____

_____

_____

_____

_____

Month

_____

Self Care Calendar

Month: _____

○ Do a 5 min breathing exercice	○ Make a feel good playlist	○ Brainstorm new activities to try	○ Watch your favourite movie	○ Listen to a podcast
○ Go for a walk	○ Declutter your space	○ Read an inspiring book	○ Write down 5 things to be happy about right now	○ Stretch out your body
○ Cook your favorite meal	○ Dance it out	○ Take a long shower or bubble bath	○ Enjoy your favorite beverage	○ Ask someone about their day
○ Have a pamper session	○ Call a friend	○ Have a digital detox day	○ Make time for creativity	○ Write down your thoughts & feelings
○ Say affirmations out loud	○ Indulge in your favorite food	○ Compliment someone	○ Write down 3 things you love about yourself	○ Enjoy a meal distraction free
○ Drink more water today	○ Try a new workout	○ Clean out a junk drawer	○ Sleep in or go to bed early	○ Celebrate a small win

Thought Tracker

Worrying about the Future

In this exercice, be mindful of every time you find your mind dwelling in the future, worrying about an event or situation that may or may not happen. If this is a legitimate problem that needs addressing, devote time to it to find a solution, but if this is a thought that is a result of fear or worry, fill out an entry in this journal table.

Thought/Worry	Is this something that is for sure going to happen?	What, if anything, can be done about it?
	◯ Yes ◯ No ◯ Maybe	
	◯ Yes ◯ No ◯ Maybe	
	◯ Yes ◯ No ◯ Maybe	
	◯ Yes ◯ No ◯ Maybe	
	◯ Yes ◯ No ◯ Maybe	
	◯ Yes ◯ No ◯ Maybe	
	◯ Yes ◯ No ◯ Maybe	
	◯ Yes ◯ No ◯ Maybe	
	◯ Yes ◯ No ◯ Maybe	
	◯ Yes ◯ No ◯ Maybe	
	◯ Yes ◯ No ◯ Maybe	
	◯ Yes ◯ No ◯ Maybe	
	◯ Yes ◯ No ◯ Maybe	
	◯ Yes ◯ No ◯ Maybe	
	◯ Yes ◯ No ◯ Maybe	
	◯ Yes ◯ No ◯ Maybe	
	◯ Yes ◯ No ◯ Maybe	
	◯ Yes ◯ No ◯ Maybe	
	◯ Yes ◯ No ◯ Maybe	
	◯ Yes ◯ No ◯ Maybe	
	◯ Yes ◯ No ◯ Maybe	
	◯ Yes ◯ No ◯ Maybe	
	◯ Yes ◯ No ◯ Maybe	
	◯ Yes ◯ No ◯ Maybe	

Affirmations

Month: _____

1. _____
2. _____
3. _____
4. _____
5. _____
6. _____
7. _____
8. _____
9. _____
10. _____
11. _____
12. _____
13. _____
14. _____
15. _____
16. _____
17. _____
18. _____
19. _____
20. _____
21. _____
22. _____
23. _____
24. _____
25. _____
26. _____
27. _____
28. _____

My Resources

Month: _____

Books

_____
_____
_____
_____

Movies

_____
_____
_____
_____

Video Games

_____
_____
_____
_____

Music

_____
_____
_____
_____

TV Shows

_____
_____
_____

My Resources

Month: _____

Books

_____

_____

_____

_____

Movies

_____

_____

_____

_____

Video Games

_____

_____

_____

_____

Music

_____

_____

_____

_____

TV Shows

_____

_____

_____

_____

My Quotes

Month: _____

○ _____
○ _____
○ _____
○ _____
○ _____
○ _____
○ _____
○ _____
○ _____
○ _____
○ _____

My Quotes

Month: _____

- ○ _____
- ○ _____
- ○ _____
- ○ _____
- ○ _____
- ○ _____
- ○ _____
- ○ _____
- ○ _____
- ○ _____
- ○ _____

My Happy Place

Month: _____

My Favorite Hobbies

- ○ _____
- ○ _____
- ○ _____
- ○ _____
- ○ _____

My Favorite Songs

- ○ _____
- ○ _____
- ○ _____
- ○ _____
- ○ _____

My Favorite Movies/TV Shows

- ○ _____
- ○ _____
- ○ _____
- ○ _____
- ○ _____

My Favorite Foods

- ○ _____
- ○ _____
- ○ _____
- ○ _____
- ○ _____

My Favorite Books

- ○ _____
- ○ _____
- ○ _____
- ○ _____
- ○ _____

My Favorite Routine

_____

_____

_____

_____

_____

Things that cheer me up

- ○ _____
- ○ _____
- ○ _____
- ○ _____
- ○ _____

Weekly Check In

Week: _____

Health: ♡ ♡ ♡ ♡ ♡		Love: ♡ ♡ ♡ ♡ ♡
Emotions: ♡ ♡ ♡ ♡ ♡		Energy: ♡ ♡ ♡ ♡ ♡
Career: ♡ ♡ ♡ ♡ ♡		Fun: ♡ ♡ ♡ ♡ ♡
Passion: ♡ ♡ ♡ ♡ ♡		Social: ♡ ♡ ♡ ♡ ♡

How am I feeling and why?

_____
_____
_____
_____
_____
_____
_____
_____

Something good about this week

_____
_____
_____
_____
_____
_____
_____
_____
_____

Something that was on my mind?

_____
_____
_____
_____
_____
_____

Stress Reduction

Week: _____

Goal #1: _____

Action Steps

○ _____   ○ _____
○ _____   ○ _____
○ _____   ○ _____
○ _____   ○ _____

Check-In / Results

Dates	Notes

Goal #2: _____

Action Steps

○ _____   ○ _____
○ _____   ○ _____
○ _____   ○ _____
○ _____   ○ _____

Check-In / Results

Dates	Notes

Positive Thinking

Week: _____

Negative Thoughts

_____

_____

_____

Is this thought true and do I have evidence that this is true

_____

_____

_____

Am I blaming someone else without taking accountability

_____

_____

_____

Am I having this thought because I'm unhappy about something else

_____

_____

_____

Positive Thoughts

_____

_____

_____

Balance Wheel

Week: _____

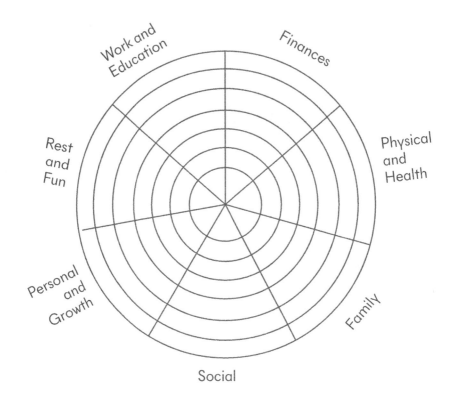

Positive Thoughts

Work and Education: _____

Finances: _____

Physical and Health: _____

Family: _____

Social: _____

Personal Growth: _____

Rest and Fun: _____

My Action Plan

Week: _____

What is your worry?

_____
_____
_____
_____
_____
_____

What is your worry trying to protect you from?

_____
_____
_____
_____
_____
_____
_____
_____
_____

What are some ways you can calm yourself with?

_____
_____
_____
_____

What action will you take to manage this worry?

_____
_____
_____

What positive result will you have from taking action?

_____
_____
_____
_____
_____
_____
_____

My Triggers

Week: _____

Why do these triggers make you feel anxious?

_____
_____
_____
_____
_____
_____
_____
_____

What are current strategies to manage these triggers?

_____
_____
_____
_____
_____
_____
_____
_____

How will you feel when you overcome these triggers?

_____
_____
_____
_____
_____
_____
_____

My Happy Place

Month: _____

My Favorite Hobbies

- ○ _____
- ○ _____
- ○ _____
- ○ _____
- ○ _____

My Favorite Songs

- ○ _____
- ○ _____
- ○ _____
- ○ _____
- ○ _____

My Favorite Movies/TV Shows

- ○ _____
- ○ _____
- ○ _____
- ○ _____
- ○ _____

My Favorite Foods

- ○ _____
- ○ _____
- ○ _____
- ○ _____
- ○ _____

My Favorite Books

- ○ _____
- ○ _____
- ○ _____
- ○ _____
- ○ _____

My Favorite Routine

_____
_____
_____
_____
_____

Things that cheer me up

- ○ _____
- ○ _____
- ○ _____
- ○ _____
- ○ _____

Weekly Check In

Week: _____

Health:	♡	♡	♡	♡	♡	Love:	♡	♡	♡	♡ ♡
Emotions:	♡	♡	♡	♡	♡	Energy:	♡	♡	♡	♡ ♡
Career:	♡	♡	♡	♡	♡	Fun:	♡	♡	♡	♡ ♡
Passion:	♡	♡	♡	♡	♡	Social:	♡	♡	♡	♡ ♡

How am I feeling and why?

_____
_____
_____
_____
_____
_____
_____
_____
_____
_____

Something good about this week

_____
_____
_____
_____
_____
_____
_____
_____
_____
_____

Something that was on my mind?

_____
_____
_____
_____
_____

Stress Reduction

Week: _____

Goal #1: _____

Action Steps

- ○ _____   ○ _____
- ○ _____   ○ _____
- ○ _____   ○ _____
- ○ _____   ○ _____

Check-In / Results

Dates	Notes

Goal #2: _____

Action Steps

- ○ _____   ○ _____
- ○ _____   ○ _____
- ○ _____   ○ _____
- ○ _____   ○ _____

Check-In / Results

Dates	Notes

Positive Thinking

Week: _____

Negative Thoughts

_____

_____

_____

Is this thought true and do I have evidence that this is true

_____

_____

_____

Am I blaming someone else without taking accountability

_____

_____

_____

Am I having this thought because I'm unhappy about something else

_____

_____

_____

Positive Thoughts

_____

_____

_____

Balance Wheel

Week: _____

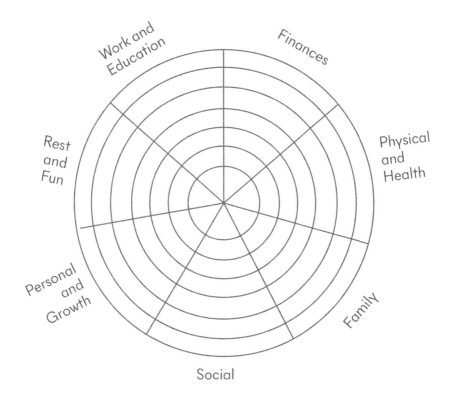

Positive Thoughts

Work and Education: _____

Finances: _____

Physical and Health: _____

Family: _____

Social: _____

Personal Growth: _____

Rest and Fun: _____

My Action Plan

Week: _____

What is your worry?

_____
_____
_____
_____
_____
_____

What are some ways you can calm yourself with?

_____
_____
_____
_____
_____

What positive result will you have from taking action?

_____
_____
_____
_____
_____
_____

What is your worry trying to protect you from?

_____
_____
_____
_____
_____
_____
_____
_____
_____

What action will you take to manage this worry?

_____
_____
_____
_____
_____
_____
_____

My Triggers

Week: _____

Why do these triggers make you feel anxious?

_____

_____

_____

_____

_____

_____

_____

What are current strategies to manage these triggers?

_____

_____

_____

_____

_____

_____

_____

How will you feel when you overcome these triggers?

_____

_____

_____

_____

_____

_____

My Happy Place

Month: _____

My Favorite Hobbies

- ○ _____
- ○ _____
- ○ _____
- ○ _____
- ○ _____

My Favorite Songs

- ○ _____
- ○ _____
- ○ _____
- ○ _____
- ○ _____

My Favorite Movies/TV Shows

- ○ _____
- ○ _____
- ○ _____
- ○ _____
- ○ _____

My Favorite Foods

- ○ _____
- ○ _____
- ○ _____
- ○ _____
- ○ _____

My Favorite Books

- ○ _____
- ○ _____
- ○ _____
- ○ _____
- ○ _____

My Favorite Routine

_____
_____
_____
_____
_____
_____
_____

Things that cheer me up

- ○ _____
- ○ _____
- ○ _____
- ○ _____
- ○ _____

Weekly Check In

Week: _____

Health: ♡ ♡ ♡ ♡ ♡   Love: ♡ ♡ ♡ ♡ ♡

Emotions: ♡ ♡ ♡ ♡ ♡   Energy: ♡ ♡ ♡ ♡ ♡

Career: ♡ ♡ ♡ ♡ ♡   Fun: ♡ ♡ ♡ ♡ ♡

Passion: ♡ ♡ ♡ ♡ ♡   Social: ♡ ♡ ♡ ♡ ♡

How am I feeling and why?

_____
_____
_____
_____
_____
_____
_____
_____
_____
_____

Something good about this week

_____
_____
_____
_____
_____
_____
_____
_____
_____
_____
_____
_____

Something that was on my mind?

_____
_____
_____
_____
_____

Stress Reduction

Week: _____

Goal #1: _____

Action Steps

○ _____   ○ _____
○ _____   ○ _____
○ _____   ○ _____
○ _____   ○ _____

Check-In / Results

Dates	Notes

Goal #2: _____

Action Steps

○ _____   ○ _____
○ _____   ○ _____
○ _____   ○ _____
○ _____   ○ _____

Check-In / Results

Dates	Notes

Positive Thinking

Week: _____

Negative Thoughts

_____
_____
_____

Is this thought true and do I have evidence that this is true

_____
_____
_____

Am I blaming someone else without taking accountability

_____
_____
_____

Am I having this thought because I'm unhappy about something else

_____
_____
_____

Positive Thoughts

_____
_____
_____

Balance Wheel

Week: _____

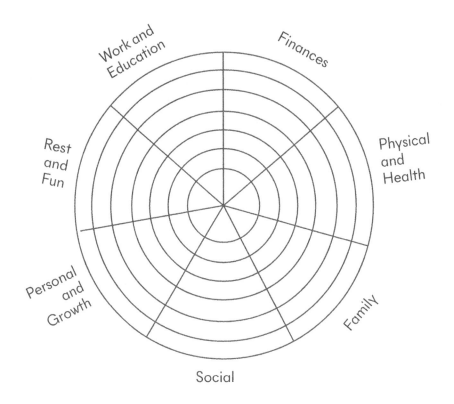

Positive Thoughts

Work and Education: _____

Finances: _____

Physical and Health: _____

Family: _____

Social: _____

Personal Growth: _____

Rest and Fun: _____

My Action Plan

Week: _____

What is your worry?

_____
_____
_____
_____
_____
_____
_____

What is your worry trying to protect you from?

_____
_____
_____
_____
_____
_____
_____
_____
_____
_____

What are some ways you can calm yourself with?

_____
_____
_____
_____
_____

What action will you take to manage this worry?

_____
_____

What positive result will you have from taking action?

_____
_____
_____
_____
_____
_____
_____

My Triggers

Week: _____

Why do these triggers make you feel anxious?

_____
_____
_____
_____
_____
_____
_____

What are current strategies to manage these triggers?

_____
_____
_____
_____
_____
_____
_____

How will you feel when you overcome these triggers?

_____
_____
_____
_____
_____
_____
_____

My Happy Place

Month: _____

My Favorite Hobbies

- ○ ....
- ○ ....
- ○ ....
- ○ ....
- ○ ....

My Favorite Songs

- ○ ....
- ○ ....
- ○ ....
- ○ ....
- ○ ....

My Favorite Movies/TV Shows

- ○ ....
- ○ ....
- ○ ....
- ○ ....
- ○ ....

My Favorite Foods

- ○ ....
- ○ ....
- ○ ....
- ○ ....
- ○ ....

My Favorite Books

- ○ ....
- ○ ....
- ○ ....
- ○ ....
- ○ ....

My Favorite Routine

Things that cheer me up

- ○ ....
- ○ ....
- ○ ....
- ○ ....
- ○ ....

Weekly Check In

Week: _____

Health: ♡ ♡ ♡ ♡ ♡   Love: ♡ ♡ ♡ ♡ ♡

Emotions: ♡ ♡ ♡ ♡ ♡   Energy: ♡ ♡ ♡ ♡ ♡

Career: ♡ ♡ ♡ ♡ ♡   Fun: ♡ ♡ ♡ ♡ ♡

Passion: ♡ ♡ ♡ ♡ ♡   Social: ♡ ♡ ♡ ♡ ♡

How am I feeling and why?

_____
_____
_____
_____
_____
_____
_____
_____
_____
_____

Something good about this week

_____
_____
_____
_____
_____
_____
_____
_____
_____
_____
_____
_____
_____

Something that was on my mind?

_____
_____
_____
_____
_____
_____
_____

Stress Reduction

Week: _____

Goal #1: _____

Action Steps

○ _____   ○ _____
○ _____   ○ _____
○ _____   ○ _____
○ _____   ○ _____

Check-In / Results

Dates	Notes

Goal #2: _____

Action Steps

○ _____   ○ _____
○ _____   ○ _____
○ _____   ○ _____
○ _____   ○ _____

Check-In / Results

Dates	Notes

Positive Thinking

Week: _____

Negative Thoughts

_____

_____

_____

Is this thought true and do I have evidence that this is true

_____

_____

_____

Am I blaming someone else without taking accountability

_____

_____

_____

Am I having this thought because I'm unhappy about something else

_____

_____

_____

Positive Thoughts

_____

_____

_____

Balance Wheel

Week: _____

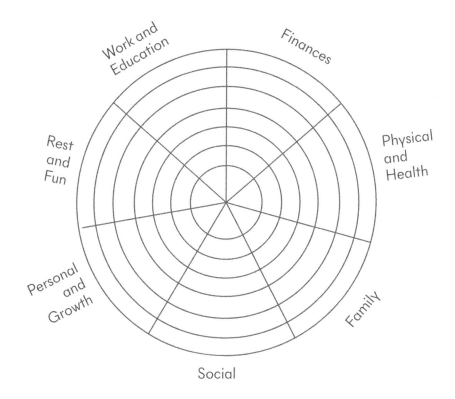

Positive Thoughts

Work and Education: _____

Finances: _____

Physical and Health: _____

Family: _____

Social: _____

Personal Growth: _____

Rest and Fun: _____

My Action Plan

Week: _____

What is your worry?

_____
_____
_____
_____
_____
_____

What is your worry trying to protect you from?

_____
_____
_____
_____
_____
_____
_____
_____

What are some ways you can calm yourself with?

_____
_____
_____
_____
_____

What action will you take to manage this worry?

_____
_____
_____

What positive result will you have from taking action?

_____
_____
_____
_____
_____
_____

My Triggers

Week: _____

Why do these triggers make you feel anxious?

_____
_____
_____
_____
_____
_____
_____
_____

What are current strategies to manage these triggers?

_____
_____
_____
_____
_____
_____
_____
_____

How will you feel when you overcome these triggers?

_____
_____
_____
_____
_____
_____

Month

Self Care Calendar

Month: _____

○ Do a 5 min breathing exercice	○ Make a feel good playlist	○ Brainstorm new activities to try	○ Watch your favourite movie	○ Listen to a podcast
○ Go for a walk	○ Declutter your space	○ Read an inspiring book	○ Write down 5 things to be happy about right now	○ Stretch out your body
○ Cook your favorite meal	○ Dance it out	○ Take a long shower or bubble bath	○ Enjoy your favorite beverage	○ Ask someone about their day
○ Have a pamper session	○ Call a friend	○ Have a digital detox day	○ Make time for creativity	○ Write down your thoughts & feelings
○ Say affirmations out loud	○ Indulge in your favorite food	○ Compliment someone	○ Write down 3 things you love about yourself	○ Enjoy a meal distraction free
○ Drink more water today	○ Try a new workout	○ Clean out a junk drawer	○ Sleep in or go to bed early	○ Celebrate a small win

Thought Tracker

Month: _____

Worrying about the Future

In this exercice, be mindful of every time you find your mind dwelling in the future, worrying about an event or situation that may or may not happen. If this is a legitimate problem that needs addressing, devote time to it to find a solution, but if this is a thought that is a result of fear or worry, fill out an entry in this journal table.

Thought/Worry	Is this something that is for sure going to happen?	What, if anything, can be done about it?
	○ Yes ○ No ○ Maybe	
	○ Yes ○ No ○ Maybe	
	○ Yes ○ No ○ Maybe	
	○ Yes ○ No ○ Maybe	
	○ Yes ○ No ○ Maybe	
	○ Yes ○ No ○ Maybe	
	○ Yes ○ No ○ Maybe	
	○ Yes ○ No ○ Maybe	
	○ Yes ○ No ○ Maybe	
	○ Yes ○ No ○ Maybe	
	○ Yes ○ No ○ Maybe	
	○ Yes ○ No ○ Maybe	
	○ Yes ○ No ○ Maybe	
	○ Yes ○ No ○ Maybe	
	○ Yes ○ No ○ Maybe	
	○ Yes ○ No ○ Maybe	
	○ Yes ○ No ○ Maybe	
	○ Yes ○ No ○ Maybe	
	○ Yes ○ No ○ Maybe	
	○ Yes ○ No ○ Maybe	
	○ Yes ○ No ○ Maybe	
	○ Yes ○ No ○ Maybe	
	○ Yes ○ No ○ Maybe	
	○ Yes ○ No ○ Maybe	
	○ Yes ○ No ○ Maybe	

Affirmations

Month: _____

1. _____
2. _____
3. _____
4. _____
5. _____
6. _____
7. _____
8. _____
9. _____
10. _____
11. _____
12. _____
13. _____
14. _____
15. _____
16. _____
17. _____
18. _____
19. _____
20. _____
21. _____
22. _____
23. _____
24. _____
25. _____
26. _____
27. _____
28. _____

My Resources

Month: _____

Books

_____
_____
_____
_____

Movies

_____
_____
_____
_____

Video Games

_____
_____
_____
_____

Music

_____
_____
_____

TV Shows

_____
_____
_____

My Resources

Month: _____

Books

Movies

Video Games

Music

TV Shows

My Quotes

Month: _____

- ○ _____
- ○ _____
- ○ _____
- ○ _____
- ○ _____
- ○ _____
- ○ _____
- ○ _____
- ○ _____
- ○ _____
- ○ _____

My Quotes

Month: _____

○ ─────────────────────────────────
○ ─────────────────────────────────
○ ─────────────────────────────────
○ ─────────────────────────────────
○ ─────────────────────────────────
○ ─────────────────────────────────
○ ─────────────────────────────────
○ ─────────────────────────────────
○ ─────────────────────────────────
○ ─────────────────────────────────
○ ─────────────────────────────────

My Happy Place

Month: _____

My Favorite Hobbies

○ _____
○ _____
○ _____
○ _____
○ _____

My Favorite Songs

○ _____
○ _____
○ _____
○ _____
○ _____

My Favorite Movies/TV Shows

○ _____
○ _____
○ _____
○ _____
○ _____

My Favorite Foods

○ _____
○ _____
○ _____
○ _____
○ _____

My Favorite Books

○ _____
○ _____
○ _____
○ _____
○ _____

My Favorite Routine

_____
_____
_____
_____
_____
_____
_____
_____
_____
_____

Things that cheer me up

○ _____
○ _____
○ _____
○ _____
○ _____

Weekly Check In

Week: _____

Health: ♡ ♡ ♡ ♡ ♡	Love: ♡ ♡ ♡ ♡ ♡
Emotions: ♡ ♡ ♡ ♡ ♡	Energy: ♡ ♡ ♡ ♡ ♡
Career: ♡ ♡ ♡ ♡ ♡	Fun: ♡ ♡ ♡ ♡ ♡
Passion: ♡ ♡ ♡ ♡ ♡	Social: ♡ ♡ ♡ ♡ ♡

How am I feeling and why?

_____
_____
_____
_____
_____
_____
_____
_____
_____

Something good about this week

_____
_____
_____
_____
_____
_____
_____
_____
_____
_____
_____
_____
_____

Something that was on my mind?

_____
_____
_____
_____

Stress Reduction

Week: _____

Goal #1: _____

Action Steps

○ _____   ○ _____
○ _____   ○ _____
○ _____   ○ _____
○ _____   ○ _____

Check-In / Results

Dates	Notes

Goal #2: _____

Action Steps

○ _____   ○ _____
○ _____   ○ _____
○ _____   ○ _____
○ _____   ○ _____

Check-In / Results

Dates	Notes

Positive Thinking

Week: _____

Negative Thoughts

_____
_____
_____
_____

Is this thought true and do I have evidence that this is true

_____
_____
_____

Am I blaming someone else without taking accountability

_____
_____
_____

Am I having this thought because I'm unhappy about something else

_____
_____
_____

Positive Thoughts

_____
_____
_____

Balance Wheel

Week: _____

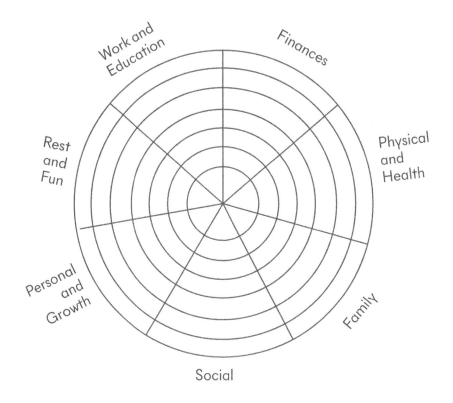

Positive Thoughts

Work and Education: _____

Finances: _____

Physical and Health: _____

Family: _____

Social: _____

Personal Growth: _____

Rest and Fun: _____

My Action Plan

Week: _____

What is your worry?

_____
_____
_____
_____
_____
_____

What is your worry trying to protect you from?

_____
_____
_____
_____
_____
_____
_____
_____
_____

What are some ways you can calm yourself with?

_____
_____
_____
_____
_____

What action will you take to manage this worry?

What positive result will you have from taking action?

_____
_____
_____
_____
_____
_____
_____

My Triggers

Week: _____

Why do these triggers make you feel anxious?

_____
_____
_____
_____
_____
_____
_____

What are current strategies to manage these triggers?

_____
_____
_____
_____
_____
_____
_____

How will you feel when you overcome these triggers?

_____
_____
_____
_____
_____
_____

My Happy Place

Month: _____

My Favorite Hobbies

- ◯ _____
- ◯ _____
- ◯ _____
- ◯ _____
- ◯ _____

My Favorite Songs

- ◯ _____
- ◯ _____
- ◯ _____
- ◯ _____
- ◯ _____

My Favorite Movies/TV Shows

- ◯ _____
- ◯ _____
- ◯ _____
- ◯ _____
- ◯ _____

My Favorite Foods

- ◯ _____
- ◯ _____
- ◯ _____
- ◯ _____
- ◯ _____

My Favorite Books

- ◯ _____
- ◯ _____
- ◯ _____
- ◯ _____
- ◯ _____

My Favorite Routine

_____
_____
_____
_____
_____
_____
_____
_____
_____

Things that cheer me up

- ◯ _____
- ◯ _____
- ◯ _____
- ◯ _____
- ◯ _____

Weekly Check In

Week: _____

Health:	♡ ♡ ♡ ♡ ♡	Love:	♡ ♡ ♡ ♡ ♡
Emotions:	♡ ♡ ♡ ♡ ♡	Energy:	♡ ♡ ♡ ♡ ♡
Career:	♡ ♡ ♡ ♡ ♡	Fun:	♡ ♡ ♡ ♡ ♡
Passion:	♡ ♡ ♡ ♡ ♡	Social:	♡ ♡ ♡ ♡ ♡

How am I feeling and why?

_____
_____
_____
_____
_____
_____
_____
_____
_____
_____

Something good about this week

_____
_____
_____
_____
_____
_____
_____
_____
_____
_____
_____
_____
_____
_____
_____
_____

Something that was on my mind?

_____
_____
_____
_____

Stress Reduction

Week: _____

Goal #1: ....

Action Steps

○ .... ○ ....
○ .... ○ ....
○ .... ○ ....
○ .... ○ ....

Check-In / Results

Dates	Notes

Goal #2: ....

Action Steps

○ .... ○ ....
○ .... ○ ....
○ .... ○ ....
○ .... ○ ....

Check-In / Results

Dates	Notes

Positive Thinking

Week: _____

Negative Thoughts

_____

_____

_____

Is this thought true and do I have evidence that this is true

_____

_____

_____

Am I blaming someone else without taking accountability

_____

_____

_____

Am I having this thought because I'm unhappy about something else

_____

_____

_____

Positive Thoughts

_____

_____

_____

Balance Wheel

Week: _____

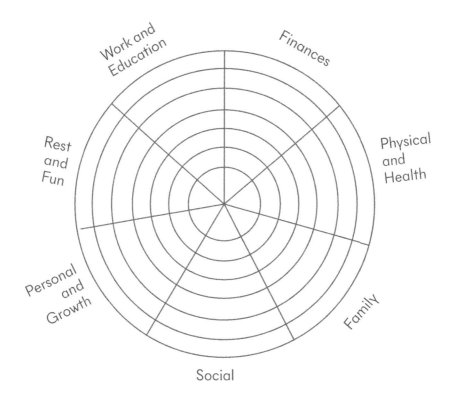

Positive Thoughts

Work and Education: _____

Finances: _____

Physical and Health: _____

Family: _____

Social: _____

Personal Growth: _____

Rest and Fun: _____

My Action Plan

What is your worry?

_____
_____
_____
_____
_____
_____

What is your worry trying to protect you from?

_____
_____
_____
_____
_____
_____
_____
_____
_____
_____

What are some ways you can calm yourself with?

_____
_____
_____
_____
_____
_____

What action will you take to manage this worry?

_____
_____
_____

What positive result will you have from taking action?

_____
_____
_____
_____
_____
_____
_____

My Triggers

Week: _____

Why do these triggers make you feel anxious?

_____

_____

_____

_____

_____

_____

_____

What are current strategies to manage these triggers?

_____

_____

_____

_____

_____

_____

_____

How will you feel when you overcome these triggers?

_____

_____

_____

_____

_____

_____

_____

My Happy Place

Month: _____

My Favorite Hobbies

- ○ _____
- ○ _____
- ○ _____
- ○ _____
- ○ _____

My Favorite Songs

- ○ _____
- ○ _____
- ○ _____
- ○ _____
- ○ _____

My Favorite Movies/TV Shows

- ○ _____
- ○ _____
- ○ _____
- ○ _____
- ○ _____

My Favorite Foods

- ○ _____
- ○ _____
- ○ _____
- ○ _____
- ○ _____

My Favorite Books

- ○ _____
- ○ _____
- ○ _____
- ○ _____
- ○ _____

My Favorite Routine

_____
_____
_____
_____
_____
_____
_____

Things that cheer me up

- ○ _____
- ○ _____
- ○ _____
- ○ _____
- ○ _____

Weekly Check In

Week: _____

Health: ♡ ♡ ♡ ♡ ♡	Love: ♡ ♡ ♡ ♡ ♡
Emotions: ♡ ♡ ♡ ♡ ♡	Energy: ♡ ♡ ♡ ♡ ♡
Career: ♡ ♡ ♡ ♡ ♡	Fun: ♡ ♡ ♡ ♡ ♡
Passion: ♡ ♡ ♡ ♡ ♡	Social: ♡ ♡ ♡ ♡ ♡

How am I feeling and why?

_____
_____
_____
_____
_____
_____
_____
_____
_____

Something good about this week

_____
_____
_____
_____
_____
_____
_____
_____
_____
_____
_____

Something that was on my mind?

_____
_____
_____
_____

Stress Reduction

Week: _____

Goal #1: _____

Action Steps

○ _____ ○ _____
○ _____ ○ _____
○ _____ ○ _____
○ _____ ○ _____

Check-In / Results

Dates	Notes

Goal #2: _____

Action Steps

○ _____ ○ _____
○ _____ ○ _____
○ _____ ○ _____
○ _____ ○ _____

Check-In / Results

Dates	Notes

Positive Thinking

Week: _____

Negative Thoughts

_____

_____

_____

Is this thought true and do I have evidence that this is true

_____

_____

_____

Am I blaming someone else without taking accountability

_____

_____

_____

Am I having this thought because I'm unhappy about something else

_____

_____

_____

Positive Thoughts

_____

_____

_____

Balance Wheel

Week: _____

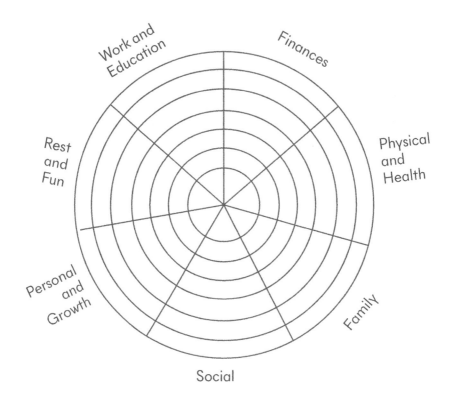

Positive Thoughts

Work and Education: _____

Finances: _____

Physical and Health: _____

Family: _____

Social: _____

Personal Growth: _____

Rest and Fun: _____

My Action Plan

Week: _____

What is your worry?

_____
_____
_____
_____
_____
_____
_____

What is your worry trying to protect you from?

_____
_____
_____
_____
_____
_____
_____
_____

What are some ways you can calm yourself with?

_____
_____
_____
_____

What action will you take to manage this worry?

_____
_____

What positive result will you have from taking action?

_____
_____
_____
_____
_____
_____
_____

My Triggers

Week: _____

Why do these triggers make you feel anxious?

_____
_____
_____
_____
_____
_____
_____

What are current strategies to manage these triggers?

_____
_____
_____
_____
_____
_____
_____

How will you feel when you overcome these triggers?

_____
_____
_____
_____
_____
_____
_____

My Happy Place

Month: _____

My Favorite Hobbies

○ ....
○ ....
○ ....
○ ....
○ ....

My Favorite Songs

○ ....
○ ....
○ ....
○ ....
○ ....

My Favorite Movies/TV Shows

○ ....
○ ....
○ ....
○ ....
○ ....

My Favorite Foods

○ ....
○ ....
○ ....
○ ....
○ ....

My Favorite Books

○ ....
○ ....
○ ....
○ ....
○ ....

My Favorite Routine

....
....
....
....
....

Things that cheer me up

○ ....
○ ....
○ ....
○ ....
○ ....

Weekly Check In

Week: _____

Health: ♡ ♡ ♡ ♡ ♡		Love: ♡ ♡ ♡ ♡ ♡
Emotions: ♡ ♡ ♡ ♡ ♡		Energy: ♡ ♡ ♡ ♡ ♡
Career: ♡ ♡ ♡ ♡ ♡		Fun: ♡ ♡ ♡ ♡ ♡
Passion: ♡ ♡ ♡ ♡ ♡		Social: ♡ ♡ ♡ ♡ ♡

How am I feeling and why?

_____
_____
_____
_____
_____
_____
_____
_____
_____
_____

Something good about this week

_____
_____
_____
_____
_____
_____
_____
_____
_____
_____
_____
_____
_____

Something that was on my mind?

_____
_____
_____
_____
_____

Stress Reduction

Week: _____

Goal #1: _____

Action Steps

○ _____   ○ _____
○ _____   ○ _____
○ _____   ○ _____
○ _____   ○ _____

Check-In / Results

Dates	Notes

Goal #2: _____

Action Steps

○ _____   ○ _____
○ _____   ○ _____
○ _____   ○ _____
○ _____   ○ _____

Check-In / Results

Dates	Notes

Positive Thinking

Week: _____

Negative Thoughts

_____
_____
_____

Is this thought true and do I have evidence that this is true

_____
_____
_____

Am I blaming someone else without taking accountability

_____
_____
_____

Am I having this thought because I'm unhappy about something else

_____
_____
_____

Positive Thoughts

_____
_____
_____

Balance Wheel

Week: _____

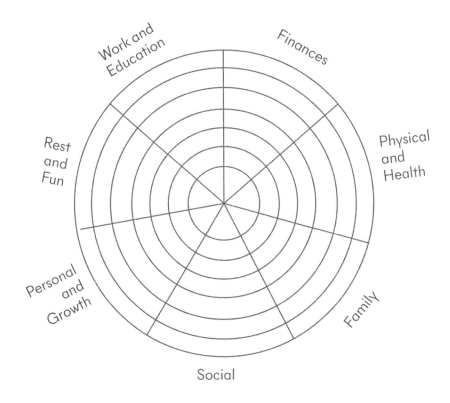

Positive Thoughts

Work and Education: _____

Finances: _____

Physical and Health: _____

Family: _____

Social: _____

Personal Growth: _____

Rest and Fun: _____

My Action Plan

Week: _____

What is your worry?

_____
_____
_____
_____
_____
_____
_____

What is your worry trying to protect you from?

_____
_____
_____
_____
_____
_____
_____
_____
_____
_____
_____

What are some ways you can calm yourself with?

_____
_____
_____
_____
_____
_____

What action will you take to manage this worry?

_____
_____
_____
_____

What positive result will you have from taking action?

_____
_____
_____
_____
_____
_____
_____

My Triggers

Week: _____

Why do these triggers make you feel anxious?

_____
_____
_____
_____
_____
_____

What are current strategies to manage these triggers?

_____
_____
_____
_____
_____
_____

How will you feel when you overcome these triggers?

_____
_____
_____
_____

Notes

Notes

Notes

Notes

Notes

Notes

Notes

Notes

Notes

Notes